The Best of Both Worlds

In this book we present two of our finest yarns, Mechita and Sock, both fingering weight, making them interchangeable for each of these 15 projects.

Mechita is a single-ply yarn, giving a wonderful soft feel with incredible drape and taking to hand dyeing beautifully. This yarn will make stunning shawls, scarves, garments, and accessories.

Sock is a soft, smoothly plied yarn that has extra stitch definition and strength. Don't be fooled by the name—while it's certainly a treat for the feet, this delightful yarn is also a particular favorite for shawls and scarves!

These luxurious yarns are made from 100% Uruguayan superwash merino wool for easy care.

Our wools are from sheep raised in Uruguay, a beautiful country with a long history of hand crafting, and with stunning landscapes that are the inspiration for our rich and striking palettes.

With more than 100 semi-solids and multi-colors in both yarns, including the new impressionist (speckled) dyes in Mechita, the possibilities for personalizing your project are endless!

Beresford

VORTEX SHAWL

Designed by Wei Wilkins

EXPERIENCED

YARN
Mechita by Malabrigo, 3½oz/100g hanks,
each approx 420yd/384m (superwash merino wool)
• 2 hanks in #036 Pearl (A)
• 1 hank each in #421 Teal Feather (B)
and #57 English Rose (C)

NEEDLES
• One each size 4 (3.5mm) circular needle,
24"/60cm and 40"/100cm long
OR SIZE TO OBTAIN GAUGE
• One size 2 (2.75 mm) circular needle, 40"/100cm long

NOTIONS
• Stitch markers
• Tapestry needle

MEASUREMENTS
Length (at top edge) 66"/167.5cm
Depth (at the point) 19"/48cm

GAUGE
24 sts and 36 rows = 4"/10cm over pat st
using size 4 (3.5mm) needle.
TAKE TIME TO CHECK YOUR GAUGE.

NOTE
This shawl is constructed by beginning at the top and
center of a base skewed shape triangle. There will be an
additional increase on the left side every 6th row (on a WS
row) for 29 more sts total at the end of this triangle shape
on this side then, as sts on the left side of this triangle are
bound off, sts along the right side of this triangle will com-
bine to be worked with 4 sets of diminished stair steps.

STITCH GLOSSARY
M1 Make 1 st by lifting the horizontal strand between st
just knit and next st, then k1tbl into this st to M1.
M1-PURL M1-purl st by lifting the horizontal strand
between st just knit and next st, then p1 into
this st to M1-purl.
M3 (K1, yo, k1) all into 1 st to make 3 sts from one st.
KFB K into front and back of st (to inc 1 st).
KBF K into back and front of st (to inc 1 st).

LITTLE KNOT STITCH
ROW 1 (RS) *M3, sl 1 wyib; rep from * to end.
ROW 2 *Sl 1 wyib, k3tog; rep from * to end.

SHORT ROW WRAP & TURN (W&T)
on RS row (on WS row)
1. Wyib (wyif), sl next st purlwise.
2. Move yarn between the needles to the front (back).
3. Sl the same st back to LH needle. Turn work.
One st is wrapped.
4. When working the wrapped st, insert RH needle under the wrap and work it tog with the corresponding st on needle.

SHAWL
TRIANGLE
With shorter size 4 (3.5 mm) circular needle and A, beg at the top center of the triangle, cast on 3 sts. Purl 1 row.
ROW 1 (RS) With A, k1, M1, (k1, yo, k1) into next st, M1, k1—7 sts.
ROW 2 P4, pm, p3.
ROW 3 K1, M1, k2, M1, sl marker, k1, M1, k2, M1, k1—11 sts.
ROW 4 P1, M1-purl, p to end—12 sts.
ROW 5 K1, M1, k to marker, M1, sl marker, k1, M1, k to last st, end M1, k1—16 sts.
ROW 6 Knit.
*ROW 7 (RS)** K1, M1, k to marker, M1, sl marker, k1, M1, k to last st, end M1, k1—4 sts inc'd.
ROW 8 Purl.
ROW 9 Rep row 7.
ROW 10 P1, M1-purl, p to 1 st before marker, M1-purl, p1, sl marker, M1-purl, p to end—3 sts inc'd.
ROW 11 With B, k1, M1, k1, *M3, sl 1 wyib, rep from * to last st, end M1, k1.
ROW 12 With B, k2, *sl 1 wyib, k3tog; rep from * to last 3 sts, end sl 1, k2.
At this point, carry B up along the side edge and twist every few rows with working color A.
ROW 13 With A, k1, M1, k to 1 st before marker, kbf, sl marker, k1, kfb, k to last st, end M1, k1—4 sts inc'd.
ROW 14 Purl.
ROW 15 K1, M1, k to marker, M1, sl marker, k1, M1, k to last st, end M1, k1—4 sts inc'd.
ROW 16 P1, M1-purl, p to end—1 st inc'd.
ROW 17 P1, M1-purl, p to marker, M1-purl, sl marker, p1, M1-purl, p to last st, end M1-purl, p1—4 sts inc'd.
ROW 18 Purl.*
Rep between *'s 12 times more, then work rows 7–9 once more—362 sts after the last inc row.
NEXT ROW (WS) P1, M1-purl, p to marker, k to end.
NEXT ROW (RS) Bind off 168 sts knitwise—195 sts rem.

BEGIN C STRIPE
ROW 1 (RS) With C, k1, k2tog, sl 1, *M3, sl 1 wyib; rep from * to last st, end M1, k1.
ROW 2 K1, M1, k1, *sl 1 wyib, k3tog; rep from * to last 3 sts, end k2tog, k1—195 sts.
ROW 3 With A, k1, k2tog, k to last st, end M1, k1.
ROW 4 Purl to last 3 sts, end p2tog, p1.
ROW 5 With C, k1, k2tog, *M3, sl 1 wyib; rep from * to last st, end M1, k1.
ROW 6 K1, M1, k1, *sl 1 wyib, k3tog; rep from * to last 2 sts, end ssk.
ROW 7 With A, k to last st, end M1, k1.
ROW 8 Purl to last 3 sts, end p2tog, p1.
Rep the last 4 rows once more.
Then, rep rows 5 and 6 once—194 sts.
NEXT ROW (RS) With A, bind off 29 sts. Cut C.

STAIR STEP 1
ROW 1 (RS) With A, k to last st, M1, k1—166 sts.
ROW 2 Purl.
SHORT ROWS 3 AND 4 K1, k2tog, k53, w&t; purl to end.
ROW 5 K1, k2tog, k to last st, end M1, k1.
ROW 6 K1, M1, k to end.
ROW 7 K1, k2tog, k to last st, end M1, k1.
ROW 8 Purl.
SHORT ROWS 9 AND 10 K1, k2tog, k108, w&t; purl to end.
ROW 11 K1, k2tog, k to last st, end M1, k1.
ROW 12 Purl.
ROW 13 With B, k2, sl 1, *M3, sl 1 wyib; rep from * to last st, end M1, k1.
ROW 14 With B, k2, *sl 1 wyib, k3tog; rep from * to last 2 sts, end sl 1, k1.

ROW 15 With A, k1, k2tog, k to last st, end M1, k1.
ROW 16 Purl.
SHORT ROWS 17 AND 18 K1, k2tog, k53, w&t; purl to end.
ROW 19 K1, k2tog, k to last st, end M1, k1.
ROW 20 K1, M1, k to end.
ROW 21 With A, k1, k2tog, k to last st, end M1, k1.
ROW 22 Purl.
SHORT ROWS 23 AND 24 K1, k2tog, k108, w&t; purl to end.
ROW 25 K1, k2tog, k to last st, end M1, k1.
ROW 26 Purl.
ROW 27 With B, k2, sl 1, *M3, sl 1 wyib; rep from * to last st, end M1, k1.
ROW 28 With B, k2, *sl 1 wyib, k3tog; rep from * to last 2 sts, end sl 1, k1.
ROW 29 With A, k1, k2tog, k to last st, end M1, k1.
ROW 30 Purl.
SHORT ROWS 31 AND 32 K1, k2tog, k53, w&t; purl to end.
ROW 33 K1, k2tog, k to last st, end M1, k1.
ROW 34 K1, M1, k to end.
ROW 35 With A, k1, k2tog, k to last st, end M1, k1.
ROW 36 Purl.
SHORT ROWS 37 AND 38 K1, k2tog, k108, w&t; purl to end.
ROW 39 K1, k2tog, k to last st, end M1, k1.
ROW 40 Purl.
ROW 41 With C, k2, sl 1, *M3, sl 1 wyib; rep from * to last 2 (or 1) sts, end k1, M1, k1 (or M1, k1).
ROW 42 K2, *sl 1 wyib, k3tog; rep from * to last 3 sts, end sl 1, k2.
ROW 43 With A, k1, k2tog, k to last st, end M1, k1.
ROW 44 Purl.
Rep the last 4 rows twice more. Then, rep rows 41 and 42 once more**—169 sts.
NEXT ROW (RS) With A, bind off 29 sts. Cut C.

STAIR STEP 2
ROW 1 (RS) With A, k to last st, end M1, k1—141 sts.
ROW 2 Purl.
Then, cont as for stair step 1 up to **, *only*, replace the number of sts on the short rows as foll: on the first short row segment, k40 sts, w&t; purl to end. On the 2nd short segment k85, w&t; purl to end. At the end of this stair step, there are 144 sts.
NEXT ROW (RS) With A, bind off 29 sts. Cut C.

STAIR STEP 3
ROW 1 (RS) With A, k to last st, end M1, k1—116 sts.
ROW 2 Purl.
Then, cont as for stair step 1 up to **, *only* replace the number of sts on the short rows as foll:
On the first short row segment, k33 sts, w&t; purl to end.
On the 2nd short row segment, k72 sts, w&t; purl to end. At the end of this stair step, there are 119 sts.
NEXT ROW (RS) With A, bind off 29 sts. Cut C.

STAIR STEP 4
ROW 1 (RS) With A, k to last st, end M1, k1—91 sts.
ROW 2 Purl.
Then, cont as for stair step 1 up to **, *only* replace the number of sts on the short rows as foll:
On the first short row segment, k28 sts, w&t; purl to end.
On the second short row segment, k58 sts, w&t; purl to end.
At the end of this segment, bind off all sts with A, do *not* cut A.

FINISHING
Cont with A using smaller circular needle and working from the RS, pick up and k approx 3 sts for every 4 rows along the top edge of shawl.
NEXT ROW (WS) Knit.
Bind off in k1, p1 rib.
Block to measurements. Using tapestry needle, weave in ends on the WS. ◆

Campanile

CHEVRON MITTS

Designed by Laura Zukaite

EASY

YARN

Mechita by Malabrigo, 3½oz/100g hanks, each approx 420yd/384m (superwash merino wool)
• 1 hank in #416 Indiecita

NEEDLES

• One pair size 5 (3.75 mm) needles
OR SIZE TO OBTAIN GAUGE

NOTIONS

• Stitch markers
• Tapestry needle

MEASUREMENTS

• Length 9½"/24cm
• Hand circumference approx 7½"/19cm
NOTE Mitts will stretch to fit.

GAUGES

• 29 sts and 40 rows = 4"/10 cm over garter st using size 5 (3.75mm) needles.
• 19 sts = 2"/5cm over chevron panel chart, using size 5 (3.75mm) needles.
TAKE TIME TO CHECK YOUR GAUGES.

MITTS (make 2 alike)

Beg at cuff edge, cast on 63 sts.
Work in garter st (k every row) for ¾"/2cm.

BEGIN CHEVRON PANEL CHART

ROW 1 (RS) K6, pm, work chevron panel chart over 19 sts, pm, k13, pm, work chevron panel chart over 19 sts, pm, k6.
ROW 2 K6, sl marker, work chevron panel chart over 19 sts, sl marker, k13, sl marker, work chevron panel chart over 19 sts, sl marker, k6.
Rep these 2 rows until piece measures 6"/15cm from beg, end with a WS row.

BEGIN THUMB GUSSET

INC ROW 1 (RS) K6, sl marker, work chevron panel chart over 19 sts, sl marker, k6, place new (gusset) marker, M1, k1, M1, place new (gusset) marker, k6, sl marker, work chevron panel chart over 19 sts, sl marker, k6—2 sts inc'd.

ROW 2 K6, sl marker, work chevron panel chart over 19 sts, sl marker, k6, sl marker, k the gusset sts to next marker, sl marker, k6, sl marker, work chevron panel chart over 19 sts, sl marker, k6.
INC ROW 3 (RS) K6, sl marker, work chevron panel chart over 19 sts, sl marker, k6, sl gusset marker, M1, k to next gusset marker, M1, sl gusset marker, k6, sl marker, work chevron panel chart over 19 sts, sl marker, k6—2 sts inc'd.
Rep last 2 rows 8 times more—there are 21 sts between the 2 gusset markers. Then, work row 2 once more.
NEXT ROW (RS) Work as established to the first gusset marker, bind off 21 sts removing the 2 gusset markers, work as established to end.
NEXT ROW (WS) Work as established to the bound-off sts, cast on 3 sts to replace these sts, work as established to end—65 sts.
NEXT ROW (RS) K6, sl marker, work chevron panel chart over 19 sts, sl marker, k15, sl marker, work chevron panel chart over 19 sts, sl marker, k6.
Cont to work in this way (with the new added sts in garter st), for 1"/2.5cm more. Then, work in garter st on all sts for ¾"/2cm more. Bind off.

FINISHING

Using tapestry needle, sew the side seam of the mitts (the seam will fall at the outer edge of the hand). Weave in ends on the WS. Lay finished mitts on a wet terry cloth tool. Steam lightly with iron (but do *not* press fabric). Leave to dry. ◆

CHEVRON PANEL

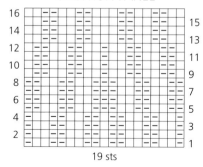

19 sts

STITCH KEY

☐ k on RS, p on WS   ⊟ p on RS, k on WS

Ardsley

ZIG-ZAG HAT

Designed by Yoko Hatta

EASY

YARN

Mechita by Malabrigo, 3½oz/100g hanks,
each approx 420yd/384m (superwash merino wool)
• 1 hank each in #412 Teal Feather (A), #811 Eggplant (B)
and #892 Pegaso (C)

NEEDLES

One set (5) each sizes 3 and 4 (3.25 and 3.5mm) dpn
OR SIZE TO OBTAIN GAUGE

NOTIONS

• Clip-on st marker
• Tapestry needle
• 2½"/6.5cm pompom marker

MEASUREMENTS

• Circumference 20½"/52cm
• Length 11½"/29cm

GAUGE

28 sts and 39 rnds = 4"/10 cm over St st
worked in rnds using size 4 (3.5mm) dpn.
TAKE TIME TO CHECK YOUR GAUGE.

NOTE

Chart pat is worked in the round in St st (k every rnd).
Read all rounds from right to left.

HAT

Beg at lower edge with smaller dpn and A, cast on 144
sts. Divide sts evenly onto dpn with 36 sts on each of the
4 dpn. Join to work in rnds, taking care not to twist sts on
needles. Use a clip-on st marker to mark beg of rnds.
RND 1 *K2, p2; rep from * around. Cont in rnds of k2,
p2 rib for 5¾"/14.5cm. Change to larger dpn
and knit 6 rnds.

BEGIN CHART PATTERN

RND 1 Work the 6-st rep for 24 reps
(or 6 reps on each of the dpn).
Cont to foll chart through rnd 18. Cut B and C. Then,
cont with A, only, knit 6 rnds.

TOP SHAPING

DEC RND 1 [K22, k2tog] 6 times—138 sts.
RND 2 Knit.
DEC RND 3 [K21, k2tog] 6 times—132 sts.
RND 4 Knit.
DEC RND 5 [K20, k2tog] 6 times—126 sts.
RND 6 Knit.
DEC RND 7 [K19, k2tog] 6 times—120 sts.
RND 8 Knit.
DEC RND 9 [K18, k2tog] 6 times—114 sts.
DEC RND 10 [K17, k2tog] 6 times—108 sts.
DEC RND 11 [K16, k2tog] 6 times—102 sts.
DEC RND 12 [K15, k2tog] 6 times—96 sts.
DEC RND 13 [K14, k2tog] 6 times—90 sts.
DEC RND 14 [K13, k2tog] 6 times—84 sts.
DEC RND 15 [K12, k2tog] 6 times—78 sts.
DEC RND 16 [K11, k2tog] 6 times—72 sts.
DEC RND 17 [K10, k2tog] 6 times—66 sts.
DEC RND 18 [K9, k2tog] 6 times—60 sts.
DEC RND 19 [K8, k2tog] 6 times—54 sts.
DEC RND 20 [K7, k2tog] 6 times—48 sts.
DEC RND 21 [K6, k2tog] 6 times—42 sts.
DEC RND 22 [K5, k2tog] 6 times—36 sts.
DEC RND 23 [K4, k2tog] 6 times—30 sts.
DEC RND 24 [K3, k2tog] 6 times—24 sts.
DEC RND 25 [K2, k2tog] 6 times—18 sts.
DEC RND 26 [K1, k2tog] 6 times—12 sts.
Cut yarn leaving a long end.

FINISHING

Thread end into tapestry needle and
draw through sts to close the top and
draw through sts a second time and pull
up securely to finish the top. Using
tapestry needle, weave in ends on the
WS. Lay finished piece on a wet terry
cloth towel. Steam lightly with iron on
back sides to measurements (but do
not press fabric). Leave to dry. Using
pompom maker and all 3 colors, make
a pompom and sew to top of hat
using the tie ends. ◆

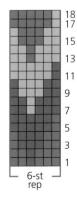

6-st
rep

COLOR KEY

■ teal feather (A) ■ eggplant (B) □ pegaso (C)

Langham

SMOOTH FREQUENCY COWL

Designed by Jacob Seifert

INTERMEDIATE

YARN

Mechita by Malabrigo, 3½oz/100g hanks, each approx 420yd/384m (superwash merino wool)
• 1 hank each in #052 Paris Night (A) and #063 Natural (B)

NEEDLES

• Size 1 (2.25mm) circular needle 24"/61cm long

NOTIONS

• 7 stitch markers in one color/style for marker 1
• 6 stitch markers in second color/style for marker 2
• 1 stitch marker in third color/style for beginning of round/marker 2
• Tapestry needle

MEASUREMENTS

• Circumference approx 20"/51cm
• Length 9½"/24cm

GAUGE

30 sts and 66 rnds to 4"/10cm over garter st using size 1 (2.25 mm) needles.
TAKE TIME TO CHECK YOUR GAUGE.

NOTES

1) When working between a marker 1 set, ignore any marker 2 in the center of the repeat. When working between a marker 2 set, ignore any marker 1 in the center of the repeat.
2) Always pick up wrapped stitches as you go.

SHORT ROW WRAP & TURN (W&T) ON RS ROW (ON WS ROW)

1. Wyib (wyif), sl next st purlwise.
2. Move yarn between the needles to the front (back).
3. Sl the same st back to LH needle. Turn work. One st is wrapped.
4. When working the wrapped st, insert RH needle under the wrap and work it tog with the corresponding st on needle.

COWL

With A, cast on 154 sts. Join, taking care to not twist stitches, and pm for beg of rnd/marker 2.
SET UP RND *K11, pm1, k11, pm2; rep from * to last 22 sts, k11, pm1, k11.
NEXT RND Purl.

BEGIN BASE HALF-OVAL

NOTE Worked between marker 2 sets.
***(RS)** K20, w&t. **(WS)** K18, w&t.
(RS) K16, w&t. **(WS)** K14, w&t.
(RS) K12, w&t. **(WS)** K10, w&t.
(RS) K8, w&t. **(WS)** K6, w&t.
(RS) K4, w&t. **(WS)** K2, w&t.
(RS) K12, w&t. **(WS)** K22, w&t.
(RS) K22, slip marker.
Rep from * to end of rnd.
NEXT RND Purl all sts.

***BEGIN STRIPE PATTERN

Join B.
***RNDS 1 AND 2** With B, knit 1 rnd, purl 1 rnd.
RNDS 3 AND 4 With A, knit 1 rnd, purl 1 rnd.
Rep from * twice more. Cut B.

BEGIN CENTERED OVAL

NOTE The center oval is worked only once, between marker 1 sets. The beg of rnd marker falls in the center of this oval.
With A, work as foll:
ROW 1 (RS) K1, w&t. **ROW 2 (WS)** K2, w&t.
ROW 3 (RS) K4, w&t. **ROW 4 (WS)** K6, w&t.
ROW 5 (RS) K8, w&t. **ROW 6 (WS)** K10, w&t.
ROW 7 (RS) K12, w&t. **ROW 8 (WS)** K14, w&t.
ROW 9 (RS) K16, w&t. **ROW 10 (WS)** K18, w&t.
ROW 11 (RS) K16, w&t. **ROW 12 (WS)** K14, w&t.
ROW 13 (RS) K12, w&t. **ROW 14 (WS)** K10, w&t.
ROW 15 (RS) K8, w&t. **ROW 16 (WS)** K6, w&t.
ROW 17 (RS) K4, w&t. **ROW 18 (WS)** K2, w&t.
ROW 19 (RS) K12, w&t. **ROW 20 (WS)** K22, w&t.
ROW 21 (RS) K22, slip marker.

BEGIN FULL OVALS

NOTE Work full ovals to end of rnd, between marker 1 sets or marker 2 sets as required by the pattern, as foll: With B, work as foll:

(RS) K12, w&t. **(WS) K2, w&t.

Work rows 3–21 same as centered oval.

Rep from ** 5 times more, ending last oval at 11 sts before end of rnd marker, purl to end of rnd.

NEXT RND Purl to 11 sts before end of rnd. Cut A. Sl 11 sts to RH needle and rejoin A for next rnd.

BEGIN STRIPE PATTERN

Work 12 rnds of stripe pat as before.

BEGIN FULL OVALS

With B, rep from ** of full oval to end of rnd—7 full ovals made.

Rep from *** until there is a total of 6 sets of stripe pat sections.

BEGIN TOP HALF-OVAL

NOTE Worked between marker 2 sets.

(RS) K12, w&t. **(WS)** K2, w&t.

(RS) K4, w&t. **(WS)** K6, w&t.

(RS) K8, w&t. **(WS)** K10, w&t.

(RS) K12, w&t. **(WS)** K14, w&t.

(RS) K16, w&t. **(WS)** K18, w&t.

(RS) K20, w&t. **(WS)** K22, w&t.

(RS) K22, slip marker.

Purl 1 rnd over all sts.

Bind off knitwise.

FINISHING

Weave in ends. Block to measurements, pin when necessary to smooth out ovals while maintaining waves in stripe sections. ◆

Leonori

YOKE PATTERNED CARDIGAN

Designed by Julie Turjoman

EXPERIENCED

SIZES
Sized for Small (Medium, Large). Shown in size Small.

YARN
Mechita by Malabrigo, 3½oz/100g hanks,
each approx 420yd/384m (superwash merino wool)
• 2 (2, 3) hanks in #892 Pegaso (A)
• 1 hank in #150 Azul Profundo (B)

NEEDLES
• One each size 4 (3.5mm) circular needle, 16" and 32"/40 and 80cm long OR SIZE TO OBTAIN GAUGE
• One set (5) size 4 (3.5mm) dpn

NOTIONS
• Stitch markers
• Tapestry needle
• Waste yarn
• Five ⅝ inch/15mm buttons
• Matching thread

MEASUREMENTS
Bust (closed) 33½ (35½, 37½)"/85 (90, 95)cm
Length 18 (18¾, 19¼)"/45.5 (47.5, 49)cm
Upper arm 13¼ (14, 15)"/33.5 (35.5, 38)cm

GAUGES
• 26 sts and 40 rows/rnds = 4"/10cm over St st using size 4 (3.5mm) needle;
• 26 sts and 38 rows = 4"/10 cm over string of pearls pattern st using size 4 (3.5mm) needle.
TAKE TIME TO CHECK YOUR GAUGES.

STRING OF PEARLS PATTERN STITCH
(worked over a multiple of 12 sts)
ROW 1 (WS) With A, purl.
ROW 2 With A, knit.
ROW 3 With A, purl.
ROW 4 (RS) With B, k11, *turn; sl 1 wyif, k3, turn; p4, k12; rep from *, end last rep k1 instead of k12.
ROW 5 With B, k5, *turn; p4, turn; k3, sl 1 wyif, k12; rep from *, end last rep k7 instead of k12.
ROW 6 With A, k8, *sl2 wyib, k10; rep from *, end last rep k2 instead of k10.

ROWS 7, 8 AND 9 With A, rep rows 1, 2 and 3.
ROW 10 (RS) With B, k5, *turn; sl 1 wyif, k3, turn; p4, k12; rep from *, end last rep k7 instead of k12.
ROW 11 With B, k11, *turn; p4, turn; k3, sl1 wyif, k12; rep from *, end last rep k1 instead of k12.
ROW 12 With A, k2, *sl2 wyib, k10; rep from *, end last rep k8 instead of k10.
ROW 13 With A, purl.
ROW 14 With A, knit.
Rep rows 1–14 for string of pearls pattern st.
Work a 24-st by 28 row swatch to familiarize yourself with the pat st before beg to knit.

NOTE Cardigan is worked from top down. Beg with shorter circular needle and change to larger circular needle when there are too many sts to fit comfortably on the needle.

BODY
Beg at the neck edge with shorter circular needle and A, cast on 120 sts. Working back and forth in rows, work as foll:
Knit 1 row, purl 1 row.
SET-UP ROW (RS) K21 (left front), pm, k18 (sleeve), pm, k42 (back), pm, k18 (sleeve), pm, k21 (right front).
NEXT ROW Purl.
RAGLAN INC ROW (RS) K to 2 sts before first marker, *kfb, k1, sl marker, kfb, k to 2 sts before next marker; rep from * 3 times more, k to end—8 sts inc'd.
Rep the last 2 rows 3 times more—152 sts.
NEXT ROW Purl.
NEXT INC ROW (This is row 4 of the pat st) work as for previous inc row, AT SAME TIME, foll row 4 of the pat st for 12 reps, pm end k8.
Cont to work the raglan inc row every other row, AT SAME TIME, working the string of pearls pat st (spacing the pearl and keeping to pat as much as possible while inc'ing) until there are 3 reps of the 14-row pat.
There are 312 sts at end of the last inc row, worked with a total of 24 raglan inc rows. Also, there are 45 sts in each front, 66 sts in each sleeve and 90 sts in the back (count 1 st at the center of each k2 that forms the raglan seam into each side of the 4 segments).
Cont in St st with A only, work the raglan inc row every

other row 5 (8, 11) times more. At end of the last row worked there are a total of 352 (376, 400) sts. Also, there are 50 (53, 56) sts in each front, 76 (82, 88) sts in each sleeve and 100 (106, 112) sts in the back.

DIVIDE FOR BODY AND SLEEVES

NEXT ROW (RS) Removing markers while working this row, k50 (53, 56) left front sts, using the backwards loop method, cast on 10 sts for the underarm, sl the next 76 (82, 88) sts of sleeve to waste yarn, k100 (106, 112) back sts, using the backwards loop method, cast on 10 sts for the underarm, sl the next 76 (82, 88) sts of sleeve to waste yarn, k50 (53, 56) right front sts—220 (232, 244) total sts.
RND 1 P55 (58, 61), pm for side seam, p110 (116, 122), pm for side seam, p55 (58, 61).
Cont in St st, work even for 2"/5cm from beg of the body.
INC ROW (RS) *K to 2 sts before side seam marker, kfb, k1, sl marker, kfb *; rep between *'s once more, then k to end —4 sts inc'd.
Rep inc row every 20 rows (or 2"/5cm) 3 times more— 236 (248, 260) sts. Work even until piece measures 11"/28 cm from beg of the body. Cut A.
NEXT ROW (RS) With B, knit.
NEXT ROW (RS) P1, *k2, p2; rep from *, end last rep p1

instead of p2. Cont in k2, p2 rib for 5 rows more. Bind off in rib.

SLEEVE

Sl the 76 (82, 88) sts on hold for one sleeve to dpn. Beg at center of the 10-st cast-on for underarm, join A and pick up and k5 sts, k the 76 (82, 88) sts, pick up and k5 sts in the underarm—86 (92, 98) sts. Join to work in rnds, divide sts onto 4 dpn and place clip-on st marker to mark beg of rnds. Work in St st (k every rnd) for 10 (6, 4) rnds.
DEC RND K1, ssk, k to last 3 sts, end k2tog, k1.
Rep dec rnd every 4th rnd 6 (7, 8) times more—72 (76, 80) sts. Work even until sleeve measures 4½"/11.5cm from the beg of the underarm. Cut A.
Knit 1 rnd with B.
NEXT RND With B, *k2, p2; rep from * around.
Cont in rnds of k2, p2 rib for 5 rnds more. Bind off in rib.
Rep for other sleeve.

NECKBAND

With RS facing, shorter circular needle and B, pick up and k14 sts along right front neck edge, 14 sts along top of sleeve, 30 sts along back neck edge, 14 sts along top of sleeve, 14 sts along left front neck edge—86 sts.

ROW 1 (WS) P2, *k2, p2; rep from * to end. Cont in k2, p2 rib for 5 rows more. Bind off in rib.

LEFT FRONT BAND

With RS facing, circular needle and B, pick up and k138 (142, 150) sts evenly along the left front edge.
ROW 1 (WS) P2, *k2, p2; rep from * to end.
Cont in k2, p2 rib for 5 rows more. Bind off in rib.

RIGHT FRONT BAND

Work as for left front band for 3 rows. On the last 3rd (WS) row, pm after the first 44 sts.
BUTTONHOLE ROW (RS) Rib to last 44 (marked) sts, [yo, p2tog, rib 8] 4 times, yo, k2tog, k2.
Rib 2 rows more. Bind off in rib.

FINISHING

Block piece to measurements. Using tapestry needle, sew in ends on the WS. Sew on buttons opposite buttonholes. ◆

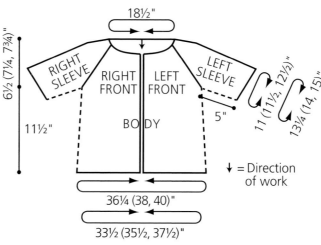

18½"

6½ (7¼, 7¾)"

RIGHT SLEEVE   RIGHT FRONT   LEFT FRONT   LEFT SLEEVE

11 (11½, 12½)"

11½"   BODY   5"   13¼ (14, 15)"

↓ = Direction of work

36¼ (38, 40)"

33½ (35½, 37½)"

Dakota

TEXTURED HAT

Designed by Karin Fernandes

INTERMEDIATE

YARN

Sock by Malabrigo, 3½oz/100g hanks,
each approx 440yd/402m (superwash merino wool)
• 1 hank each in #811 Eggplant (A) and #850 Archangel (B)

NEEDLES

• Size 1 (2.25mm) circular needle 16"/40cm long
• One set (5) size 1 (2.25mm) double-pointed needles (dpn), OR SIZE TO OBTAIN GAUGE

NOTIONS

• Four stitch markers, 1 in a unique color
• Tapestry needle

MEASUREMENTS

• Circumference (unstretched) 16 ½"/42cm*
• Length 9½"/24cm
*Note: Hat will stretch to fit.

GAUGE

39 sts and 49 rows = 4"/10cm over pat st
using size 1 (2.25mm) needles.
TAKE TIME TO CHECK YOUR GAUGE.

BRIM

With A, cast on 160 sts using the long tail cast on method. Place marker (unique color) and join to work in the round, being careful to not twist the stitches.
RND 1 Knit.
RNDS 2–9 *K1 tbl, p1; rep from * around.

BODY

SECTION 1 Cont with A as foll:
RND 1 *K3 tbl, p1; rep from * around.
RND 2 *K3, p1; rep from * around.
RNDS 3 AND 4 *P1, k3; rep from * around.
RNDS 5 AND 6 *K1, p1, k2; rep from * around.
RNDS 7 AND 8 *K2, p1, k1; rep from * around.
RNDS 9 AND 10 *K3, p1; rep from * around.
Rep rnds 3–10 twice more. Rep rnds 3 and 4 once more.

SECTION 2
RND 1 With B, *k1, p1, k2; rep from * around.
RND 2 With A, *k1, p1, k2; rep from * around.
RND 3 With B, *p1, k3; rep from * around.

RND 4 With A, *p1, k3; rep from * around.
RND 5 With B, *k3, p1; rep from * around.
RND 6 With A, *k3, p1; rep from * around.
RND 7 With B, *k2, p1, k1; rep from * around.
RND 8 With A, *k2, p1, k1; rep from * around.
Rep rnds 1–8 twice more. Rep rnds 1–4 once more. Cut A.

SECTION 3 Cont with B as foll:
RNDS 1 AND 2 *K3, p1; rep from * around.
RNDS 3 AND 4 *P1, k3; rep from * around.
RNDS 5 AND 6 *K1, p1, k2; rep from * around.
RNDS 7 AND 8 *K2, p1, k1; rep from * around.
Rep rnds 1–8 twice more. Rep rnds 1–3 once more.

CROWN SHAPING
NOTE Change to dpns when necessary.
SET-UP RND *[P1, k3] 10 times, pm; rep from * twice more, [p1, k3] 10 times.
RND 1 K1, *p1, k3; rep from * to 3 sts before next marker, k1, ssk, sm; rep from * to end of rnd—156 sts.
RND 2 K1, *p1, k3; rep from * to 2 sts before next marker, ssk, sm; rep from * to end of rnd—152 sts.
RND 3 K2, *p1, k3; rep from * to 4 sts before next marker, p1, k1, ssk, sm; rep from * to end of rnd—148 sts.
RND 4 K2, *p1, k3; rep from * to 3 sts before next marker, p1, ssk, sm; rep from * to end of rnd—144 sts.
RND 5 *K3, p1; rep from * to 4 sts before next marker, k2, ssk, sm; rep from * to end of rnd—140 sts.
RND 6 *K3, p1; rep from * to 3 sts before next marker, k1, ssk, sm; rep from * to end of rnd—136 sts.
RND 7 *P1, k3; rep from * to 2 sts before next marker, ssk, sm; rep from * to end of rnd—132 sts.
RND 8 *P1, k3 to 5 sts before next marker, p1, k2, ssk, sm; rep from * to end of rnd—128 sts.
Rep rnds 1–8 three times more—32 sts.
Rep rnds 1 and 2 once more—24 sts.
NEXT RND *K2, p1, k1, ssk, sm; rep from * around—20 sts.
LAST RND *K2, p1, ssk, sm; rep from * around—16 sts.

FINISHING

Cut yarn and thread onto tapestry needle. Draw needle through rem sts and pull taut. Secure end. With A and B, make a 1½"/4cm pom-pom and attach it to the top of the hat. Weave in the ends and block as desired. ◆

Prasada

COLORWORK CRESCENT SHAWL

Designed by Laura Zukaite

INTERMEDIATE

YARN
Sock by Malabrigo, 3½oz/100g hanks,
each approx 440yd/402m (superwash merino wool)
• 1 hank each in #855 Aguas (A), #120 Lotus (B)
and #852 Persia (C)

NEEDLES
• Size 5 (3.75mm) circular needle 40"/100cm long,
OR SIZE TO OBTAIN GAUGE
• Size F/5 (3.75mm) crochet hook

MEASUREMENTS
• Width 44"/111.5cm
• Length 19"/48cm

GAUGES
• 20 sts and 36 rows = 4"/10cm over St st
using size 5 (3.75mm) needles.
• 24 sts and 40 rows = 4"/10cm over garter st
using size 5 (3.75mm) needles.
TAKE TIME TO CHECK YOUR GAUGES.

NOTES
1. Wind bobbins for each section of A and B in chart pat,
do not strand across pattern.
2. Chart is worked in St st (k on RS, p on WS). Work 1
selvage stitch at each side in garter st (knit every row).

SHAWL
With A, cast on 322 sts.
NEXT ROW (WS) K1, p to last st, k1.

BEG CHART
ROW 1 (RS) K1, work 40-st rep 8 times, k1.
Cont to work chart in this way through row 42—290 sts.
Cut A and B and work in C only to end.

GARTER SECTION
With C, knit 10 rows.
DEC ROW 1 (RS) K1, *k2tog, k14, ssk;
rep from * to last st, k1—258 sts.
Knit 11 rows.

DEC ROW 2 (RS) K1, *k2tog, k12, ssk; rep from * to last st, k1—226 sts. Knit 11 rows.
DEC ROW 3 (RS) K1, *k2tog, k10, ssk; rep from * to last st, k1—194 sts. Knit 11 rows.
DEC ROW 4 (RS) K1, *k2tog, k8, ssk; rep from * to last st, k1—162 sts. Knit 11 rows.
DEC ROW 5 (RS) K1, *k2tog, k6, ssk; rep from * to last st, k1—130 sts. Knit 11 rows.
DEC ROW 6 (RS) K1, *k2tog, k4, ssk; rep from * to last st, k1—98 sts. Knit 11 rows.
DEC ROW 7 (RS) K1, *k2tog, k2, ssk; rep from * to last st, k1—66 sts. Knit 11 rows.

DEC ROW 8 (RS) K1, *k2tog, ssk; rep from * to last st, k1—34 sts. Knit 11 rows.
DEC ROW 9 (RS) K1, *k2tog, ssk; rep from * to last st, k1—18 sts. Knit 5 rows.
DEC ROW 10 (RS) K1, *k2tog, ssk; rep from * to last st, k1—10 sts. Cut yarn and pull through rem sts, draw up and fasten off.

FINISHING
Block lightly to measurements.
With RS facing, crochet hook and C, work a row of sc evenly along cast-on edge. Do *not* turn. Work a row of backwards sc (from left to right) in each sc. Fasten off.◆

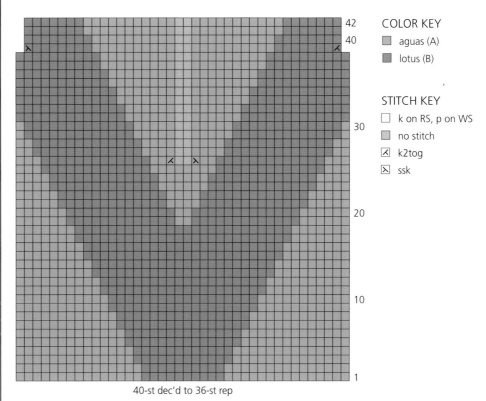

40-st dec'd to 36-st rep

COLOR KEY
☐ aguas (A)
◼ lotus (B)

STITCH KEY
☐ k on RS, p on WS
◻ no stitch
☒ k2tog
☒ ssk

Orienta

WAKE SHAWL

Designed by Cory Ellen Boberg

INTERMEDIATE

YARN

Mechita by Malabrigo, 3½oz/100g hanks,
each approx 420yd/384m (superwash merino wool)
• 2 hanks in #888 Sirenas (MC)
• 1 hank in #150 Azul Profundo (CC)

NEEDLES

• Size 6 (4mm) circular needle 32"/80cm long,
OR SIZE TO OBTAIN GAUGE

NOTIONS

• Stitch markers
• One locking stitch marker

MEASUREMENTS

• Width 76"/193cm
• Length 23"/58.5cm

GAUGE

24 sts and 50 rows = 4"/10cm over garter st
using size 6 (4mm) needle.
TAKE TIME TO CHECK YOUR GAUGE.

LATTICE LACE PAT

ROW 1 (RS) K1, *yo, ssk; rep from * to 3 sts before
marker, yo, SK2P, yo, sl marker, *k2tog, yo;
rep from * to last st, k1.
ROW 2 Kfb, p to last st, kfb—2 sts inc'd.
ROW 3 K1, *yo, ssk; rep from * to 4 sts before marker,
yo, k1, S2KP, remove marker, k1, place marker, yo, *k2tog,
yo; rep from * to last st, k1.
ROW 4 Kfb, p to last st, kfb—2 sts inc'd.
Rep rows 1–4 for lattice lace pat.

NOTE

When carrying unused color up side of work in stripe
sections, twist with working yarn at beg of every RS row
by bringing carried yarn from right to left over working
yarn, continue with working yarn.

SHAWL

With MC, cast on 5 sts using long-tail method.
NEXT ROW (WS) Kfb, place marker (pm), k3, kfb—7 sts.

BEG INCREASE GARTER SECTION

ROW 1 (RS) Kfb, k to 3 sts before marker, SK2P, remove marker, k1, place marker, k to last st, kfb.
ROW 2 (WS) Kfb, k to last st, kfb—2 sts inc'd.
Rep rows 1 and 2 for increase garter pat 14 times more—37 sts.

**STRIPE SECTION 1

ROWS 1–4 With CC, rep rows 1 and 2 of increase garter pat twice.
ROWS 5–6 With MC, rep rows 1 and 2 of increase garter pat—43 sts.
Cut MC.

LATTICE LACE SECTION

SET-UP ROW 1 (RS) With CC, rep row 1 of increase garter pat.
SET-UP ROW 2 Kfb, p to last st, kfb—45 sts.
Work rows 1–4 of lattice lace pat 3 times, then work rows 1 and 2 once more—59 sts.

STRIPE SECTION 2

ROWS 1–2 With MC, rep rows 1 and 2 of increase garter pat.
ROWS 4–6 With CC, rep rows 1 and 2 of increase garter pat twice—65 sts.
Cut CC.

INCREASE GARTER SECTION

With MC, rep rows 1 and 2 of increase garter pat 16 times—97 sts.

Rep from ** once (157 sts), then rep Stripe section 1 and Lattice lace section once more—179 sts.

FINAL INCREASE GARTER SECTION

ROWS 1–2 With MC, rep rows 1 and 2 of increase garter pat—181 sts.
ROWS 3–4 With CC, rep rows 1 and 2 of increase garter pat—183 sts.
ROW 5 With CC, rep row 1 of increase garter pat.
ROW 6 With CC, k to last st, kfb—184 sts.

EVEN BODY SECTION

EVEN ROW 1 (RS) With MC, kfb, k to 3 sts before marker, SK2P, remove marker, k1, place marker, k to end.
EVEN ROW 2 With MC, k to last st, kfb.
EVEN ROWS 3 AND 4 With MC, rep even rows 1 and 2.
EVEN ROWS 5 AND 6 With CC, rep even rows 1 and 2.
Rep even rows 1–6 for 29 times more, until no sts rem after the marker. Remove marker—184 sts. Cut CC.

NEXT ROW (RS) With MC, kfb, k to last 3 sts, SK2P—183 sts. Do not cut MC.

EDGING

NOTE Continuing along the same edge as the row just worked, edging stitches are picked up along the side edge of sts that were after the center marker.
With locking stitch marker, mark point of shawl at left edge of work. With MC, pick up and k 91 sts along upper edge to marker, picking up 1 st in each garter bump—274 sts.

Bind off all sts with MC as foll:
*k2tog tbl, slip st purlwise back to LH needle; rep from * to last st. Pull yarn through last st and fasten off.
Block to measurements. ◆

Ansonia

SCALLOPED COWL

Designed by Debbie O'Neill

EASY

YARN

Sock by Malabrigo, 3½oz/100g hanks,
each approx 440yd/402m (superwash merino wool)
• 1 hank each in #809 Solis (A)
and #851 Turner (B)

NEEDLES
• Size 3 (3.25mm) circular needle 24"/70cm long

NOTIONS
• Stitch marker
• Tapestry needle

MEASUREMENTS
• Circumference 26"/66cm
• Length 15"/38cm

GAUGE

25 sts and 36 rows = 4"/10cm over
scalloped stripe pattern after blocking
TAKE TIME TO CHECK YOUR GAUGE.

STITCH GLOSSARY

S2KP Slip 2 tog knitwise, k1,
pass 2 slipped stitches over k1.

SCALLOPED STRIPE PATTERN

(Worked over a multiple of 12 sts)
RND 1 (AND EVERY ODD RND) Knit.
RNDS 2 AND 4 Purl.
RND 6 *K1, yo, k4, S2KP, k4, yo; rep from * around.
RND 8 *K2, yo, k3, S2KP, k3, yo, k1; rep from * around.
RND 10 *K3, yo, k2, S2KP, k2, yo, k2; rep from * around.
RND 12 *K4, yo, k1, S2KP, k1, yo, k3; rep from * around.
RND 14 *K5, yo, S2KP, yo, k4; rep from * around.
RND 15 Knit.
Rep rnds 1–15 for scalloped stripe pat.

NOTES

1) To avoid weaving in multiple ends, carry yarns up along
the inside of the cowl. Take care to twist the carried yarn
with the working color every other row for a clean edge.
2) Cowl can easily be made wider by adding stitches in
multiples of 12, and made longer by working additional
15-rnd pat repeats. As written, cowl uses about
½ of each skein.
3) Scalloped stripe pat can be worked either from
chart or written instructions.

COWL

With A, cast on 180 sts loosely.
Join and pm for beg of rnd.

BEGIN PAT
*With A, work rnds 1–15 of scalloped stripe pat.
With B, work rnds 1–15 of pat; rep from * (30 rnds) three
times more. Cut B. With A, work rnds 1–15 of pat.
Bind off all sts loosely knitwise. ◆

STITCH KEY

☐ knit
⊟ purl
⊡ yo
⊼ S2KP

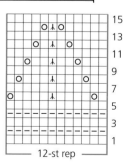

					○	⊼	○					15

— 12-st rep —

Chatsworth

CRESCENT SHAWL

Designed by Hanna Maciejewska

INTERMEDIATE

YARN

Mechita by Malabrigo, 3½oz/100g hanks, each approx 420yd/384m (superwash merino wool)
• 3 hanks in #57 English Rose

NEEDLES
• Size 4 (3.5mm) circular needle 40"/100cm long, OR SIZE TO OBTAIN GAUGE

NOTIONS
• Stitch markers

MEASUREMENTS
• Width 64"/162.5cm
• Length 16"/40.5cm

GAUGE

23 sts and 35 rows = 4"/10cm over garter st using size 4 (3.5mm) needles.
TAKE TIME TO CHECK YOUR GAUGE.

STITCH GLOSSARY

M1R Insert LH needle from back to front under the strand between last st worked and next st on LH needle. Knit into the front loop to twist the st.
M1L Insert LH needle from front to back under the strand between last st worked and next st on LH needle. Knit into the back loop to twist the st.

SHAWL

Cast on 3 sts. Knit 7 rows. Turn 90 degrees and pick up 3 sts along side edge of tab, 3 sts along cast-on edge—9 sts.
ROW 1 (RS) K3, M1L, kfb to last 3 sts, M1R, k3—14 sts.
ROW 2 K3, M1L, k to last 3 sts, M1R, k3—2 sts inc'd.
ROWS 3–9 Rep row 2—30 sts.
ROW 10 K3, M1L, [k2, M1L] 6 times, [k2, M1R] 6 times, k3—43 sts.

BODY
ROW 1 K3, M1L, k to last 3 sts, M1R, k3—2 sts inc'd.
ROWS 2 AND 3 Rep row 1.
ROW 4 K2, kfb, M1L, k to last 3 sts, M1R, kfb, k2—4 sts inc'd.
ROWS 5–12 Rep rows 1–4 twice.

ROWS 13 AND 14 Rep row 1.
ROWS 15 AND 16 Rep row 4.

Rep rows 1–16 five times more—295 sts.
Rep rows 1–4 twice more—315 sts.

NEXT 2 ROWS Rep row 1—319 sts.
NEXT 2 ROWS Rep row 4—327 sts.

BORDER
NOTE Border may be worked following text or chart.
ROW 1 K3, M1R, *k1, yo, k3, ssk, k5, k2tog, k3, yo; rep from * to last 4 sts, k1, M1L, k3.
ROW 2 K3, M1L, k2, *k1, p13, k2; rep from * to last 4 sts, k1, M1R, k3.
ROW 3 K3, M1R, k2, *k2, yo, k3, ssk, k3, k2tog, k3, yo, k1; rep from * to last 6 sts, k3, M1L, k3.
ROW 4 K2, M1L, kbf, p1, k3, *k2, p11, k3; rep from * to last 6 sts, k2, p1, pfb, M1R, k2.
ROW 5 K3, M1R, k5, *k3, yo, k3, ssk, k1, k2tog, k3, yo, k2; rep from * to last 9 sts, k6, M1L, k3.
ROW 6 K3, M1L, p3, k4, *k3, p9, k4; rep from * to last 9 sts, k3, p3, M1R, k3.
ROW 7 K3, M1R, k7, *k4, yo, k3, S2KP, k3, yo, k3; rep from * to last 11 sts, k8, M1L, k3.
ROW 8 K2, M1L, kbf, p5, k4, *k3, p9, k4; rep from * to last 11 sts, k3, p5, pfb, M1R, k2.
ROW 9 K3, M1R, k2, k2tog, k3, yo, k3, *k4, yo, k3, S2KP, k3, yo, k3; rep from * to last 14 sts, k4, yo, k3, ssk, k2, M1L, k3.
ROW 10 K3, M1L, p8, k4, *k3, p9, k4; rep from * to last 14 sts, k3, p8, M1R, k3.
ROW 11 K2, M1R, kbf, k4, k2tog, k3, yo, k3, *k4, yo, k3, S2KP, k3, yo, k3; rep from * to last 16 sts, k4, yo, k3, ssk, k4, kfb, M1L, k2.
ROW 12 K2, M1L, kbf, p to last 3 sts, pfb, M1R, k2.
ROW 13 K3, M1R, *k3, k2tog, k3, [yo, k1] twice, k2, ssk, k2; rep from * to last 4 sts, k1, M1L, k3.
ROW 14 K3, M1L, p2, *p6, k3, p7; rep from * to last 4 sts, p1, M1R, k3.
ROW 15 K3, M1R, k2, *k2, k2tog, [k3, yo] twice, k3, ssk, k1; rep from * to last 6 sts, k3, M1L, k3.
ROW 16 K2, M1L, kbf, p4, *p5, k5, p6; rep from * to last 6 sts, p3, pfb, M1R, k2.

ROW 17 K3, M1R, k5, *k1, k2tog, [k3, yo, k2] twice, k1, ssk; rep from * to last 9 sts, k6, M1L, k3.

ROW 18 K3, M1L, k2, p5, *p4, k7, p5; rep from * to last 9 sts, p4, k2, M1R, k3.

ROW 19 K3, M1R, k3, yo, k3, *S2KP, k3, yo, k7, yo, k3; rep from * to last 12 sts, S2KP, k3, yo, k3, M1L, k3.

ROW 20 K2, M1L, kbf, k4, p5, *p4, k7, p5; rep from * to last 11 sts, p4, k4, pfb, M1R, k2.

ROW 21 K3, M1R, k6, yo, k3, *S2KP, k3, yo, k7, yo, k3; rep from * to last 15 sts, S2KP, k3, yo, k6, M1L, k3.

ROW 22 K3, M1L, p1, k6, p5, *p4, k7, p5; rep from * to last 14 sts, p4, k6, p1, M1R, k3.

ROW 23 K2, M1R, kbf, k8, yo, k3, *S2KP, k3, yo, k7, yo, k3; rep from * to last 17 sts, S2KP, k3, yo, k8, kbf, M1L, k2.

ROW 24 K2, M1L, kbf, p to last 3 sts, pfb, M1R, k2. A total of 64 sts have been inc'd. Rep rows 1–24 once more—455 sts.

END BORDER

ROWS 1–3 K3, M1L, k to last 3 sts, M1R, k3—461 sts.

ROW 4 K2, kfb, M1L, k to last 3 sts, M1R, kfb, k2—465 sts.

ROW 5 K3, M1L, k to last 3 sts, M1R, k3—467 sts.

Bind off loosely, knitwise. Block to measurements. ◆

BORDER

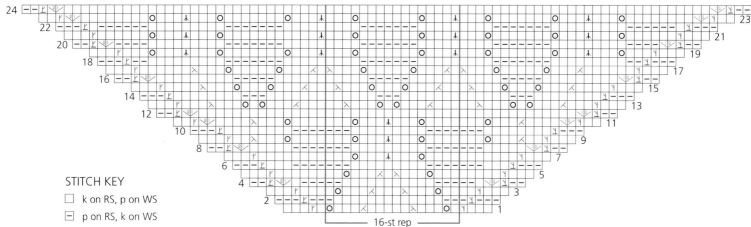

16-st rep

STITCH KEY

- ☐ k on RS, p on WS
- ⊟ p on RS, k on WS
- ⊙ yo
- ⧄ k2tog
- ⧅ ssk
- ⊼ S2KP
- M1R on RS
- M1R on WS
- M1L on RS
- M1L on WS
- kfb on RS, kbf on WS
- kbf on RS, pfb on WS

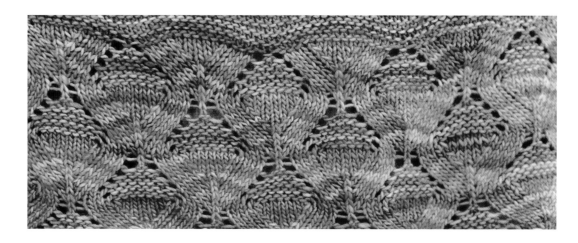

Normandy

CABLE SOCKS

Designed by Anne Jones

EXPERIENCED

SIZES

Sized for Small (Medium, Large).
Shown in size Small.

YARN

Sock by Malabrigo, 3½oz/100g hanks,
each approx 400yd/365m (superwash merino wool)
• 1 hank in #862 Piedras

NEEDLES

• Two size 1 (2.25mm) circular needles
16"/40.5cm long for size Small
• Two size 2 (2.75mm) circular needles
16"/40.5cm long for size Medium
• Two size 3 (3.25mm) circular needles
16"/40.5cm long for size Large

NOTIONS

• Stitch markers
• Cable needle (cn)
• Tapestry needle

MEASUREMENTS

TO FIT WOMAN'S SHOE SIZE 6-8 (8-10, 10-12)
• Calf circumference (blocked)
7½ (8, 8½)"/19 (20.5, 21.5)cm
• Length to beg of heel 6¾ (7, 7½)"/17 (18, 19)cm
• Length, heel to toe 9 (9¼, 9¾)"/23 (23.5, 25)cm

GAUGES (after blocking)

• 33 sts and 46 rnds = 4"/10cm over St st
using size 1 (2.25mm) needles.
• 35 sts and 44 rnds = 4"/10 cm over chart pat
using size 1 (2.25mm) needles.
• 30 sts and 44 rnds = 4"/10cm over St st
using size 2 (2.75mm) needles.
• 32 sts and 43 rnds = 4"/10cm over chart pat
using size 2 (2.75mm) needles.
• 29 sts and 42 rnds = 4"/10cm over St st
using size 3 (3.25mm) needles.
• 30 sts and 38 rnds = 4"/10cm over chart pat
using size 3 (3.25mm) needles.
TAKE TIME TO CHECK YOUR GAUGES.

STITCH GLOSSARY

4-ST LC Sl 2 sts to cable needle and hold to *front* of work;
k2, k2 from cn.
3-ST LPC Sl 2 sts to cable needle and hold to *front* of
work; p1, k2 from cn.
3-ST RC Sl 1 st to cable needle and hold to *back* of work;
k2, k1 from cn.
4-ST LC JOIN (worked when the 4 sts of a 4-st cable is
split between two different needles)
Sl last 2 unworked sts at end of last rnd from previous
needle to cable needle and hold to *front* of work. Knit 2
sts from foll needle and sl to previous needle—32 sts on
previous needle. Knit 2 sts from cable needle to foll needle.

NOTE

Socks are worked in the round on two 16"/40cm circular
needles to reduce number of cables crossed over joins. To
make it easier to distinguish the needles, use two different
colored needles or two different lengths. Pattern can be
worked on dpn if preferred.

SOCK

Using long-tail method, cast on 64 sts. Divide over two
16"/40cm circular needles (32 sts each needle) and join,
place marker for beg of rnd.
NEXT RND *K2, p2; rep from * around.
Rep last rnd for k2, p2 rib until cuff measures 1¾"/4.5cm,
working to 2 sts before end of last rnd.

BEG LEG CHART
RND 1 Work 4-st LC join (first 4 sts of chart), then cont pat
to end of rnd.

Cont in pat as established through rnd 28 of leg chart,
leaving last 2 sts of rnd 28 unworked. Rep rnds 1-28 of
leg chart once more.

HEEL FLAP

NOTE Heel flap is worked back and forth in rows.
SET-UP ROW (RS) Knit 16 sts on needle 1.
Using needle 2, knit rem 16 sts from needle 1. Knit 16 sts
on needle 2. Sl next 16 sts from needle 2 to needle 1.
Cont 32 heel sts on needle 2 only, leaving 32 sts of needle
1 on hold, as foll:

ROW 1 (RS) [Sl 1 wyib, k1] 16 times.

ROW 2 Sl 1 wyif, p31.

Rep rows 1 and 2 until heel flap measures 2¼"/5.5cm, or desired length, end with a WS row.

TURN HEEL

ROW 1 (RS) Sl 1 wyib, k17, k2tog, k1, turn.

ROW 2 Sl 1 wyif, p5, ssp, p1, turn.

ROW 3 Sl 1 wyib, k to 1 st before gap, k2tog, k1, turn.

ROW 4 Sl 1 wyif, p to 1 st before gap, ssp, p1, turn.

Rep rows 3 and 4 until 1 st rem on either side.

NEXT ROW Sl 1 wyib, k to 1 st before gap, k2tog, turn.

FINAL ROW Sl 1 wyif, p to 1 st before gap, ssp—18 sts.

GUSSET

SET-UP RND With needle 1, sl 1 wyib, k8, pm for beg of rnd, pick up and k 12 sts into slipped sts along heel flap and 1 st between heel flap and top of foot to close gap. Work row 1 from foot chart across 32 sts of needle 2. With needle 1, pickup and k 1 st between top of foot and heel flap, then pick up and k 12 into slipped sts along side of heel flap. K 9 sts to marker—76 sts.

RND 1 *Needle 1:* K to last 3 sts, k2tog, k1; *Needle 2:* Cont foot chart as established to end of needle; *Needle 1:* K1, ssk, k to end of rnd—2 sts dec'd.

RND 2 *Needle 1:* Knit; *Needle 2:* Cont foot chart as established to end of needle; *Needle 1:* Knit.

Rep last 2 rnds until 32 sts rem on each needle—64 sts.

Rep rnd 2 until foot measures 2"/5cm less than desired length from back of heel.

TOE

RND 1 *Needle 1:* K to last 3 sts, k2tog, k1; *Needle 2:* K1, ssk, k to last 3 sts, k2tog, k1; *Needle 1:* K1, ssk, k to end of rnd.

RND 2 Knit.

Rep rnds 1 and 2 until 32 sts rem.

Rep rnd 1 until 16 sts rem.

With needle 1, k first 4 sts of rnd—8 sts per needle.

Cut yarn leaving a 12"/30.5cm tail. With tapestry needle, graft to using Kitchener stitch.

Work 2nd sock in same way. ◆

LEG CHART

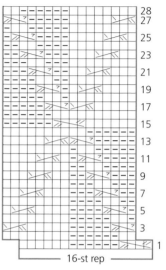

16-st rep

FOOT CHART

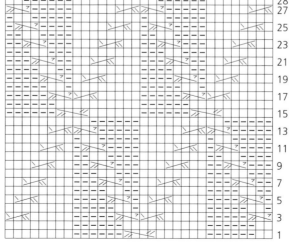

32 sts

STITCH KEY

☐ k

⊟ p

▱ 4-st LC

▱ 3-st LPC

▱ 3-st RC

Osborne

STRIPED COWL

Designed by Florence Spurling

INTERMEDIATE

YARN

Sock by Malabrigo, 3½oz/100g hanks,
each approx 440yd/402m (superwash merino wool)
• 2 hanks in #63 Natural (A)
• 1 hank each in #810 Cordovan (B)
and #801 Boticelli Red (C)

NEEDLES

• One pair size 4 (3.5mm) needles,
OR SIZE TO OBTAIN GAUGE

NOTIONS

• Tapestry needle

MEASUREMENTS

• Circumference 56"/142cm
• Width 10"/25.5cm

GAUGE

28 sts and 50 rows = 4"/10cm over seed st
using size 4 (3.5mm) needles.
TAKE TIME TO CHECK YOUR GAUGE.

SEED STITCH

(over an odd number of sts)
ROW 1 (RS) K1, *p1, k1; rep from * to end.
ROW 2 Purl the knit sts and knit the purl sts.
Rep row 2 for seed st.

COWL

With A, cast on 73 sts.
ROWS 1–14 Work in seed st.
ROW 15 (RS) With C, knit.
ROW 16 With C, k2, p to last 2 sts, k2.
ROW 17 With A, knit.
ROW 18 With A, k2, p to last 2 sts, k2.
ROWS 19 AND 20 Rep rows 15 and 16.
ROWS 21 AND 22 Rep rows 17 and 18.
ROWS 23 AND 24 Rep rows 15 and 16.
ROWS 25–38 With A, work in seed st.
ROW 39 With B, knit.
ROW 40 With B, k2, p to last 2 sts, k2.
ROW 41 With A, knit.
ROW 42 With A, k2, p to last 2 sts, k2.

ROWS 43 AND 44 Rep rows 41 and 42.
ROWS 45 AND 46 With B, knit.
ROW 47 With C, k1, *sl 1 wyib, k1; rep from * to end.
ROW 48 With C, k1, *sl 1 wyif, k1; rep from * to end.
ROWS 49 AND 50 With B, knit.
ROW 51 With A, k2, *sl 1 wyib, k1;
rep from * to last st, k1.
ROW 52 With A, k2, *sl 1 wyif, p1;
rep from * to last 3 sts, sl 1 wyif, k2.
ROWS 53–56 Rep rows 41 and 42 twice.
ROWS 57 AND 58 Rep rows 39 and 40.
ROWS 59–72 With A, work in seed st.
ROW 73 With B, knit.
ROW 74 With B, k2, p to last 2 sts, k2.
ROW 75 With A, knit.
ROW 76 With A, k2, p to last 2 sts, k2.
ROWS 77–80 Rep rows 73–76.
ROWS 81 AND 82 Rep rows 73 and 74.
ROWS 83–96 With A, work in seed st.
ROW 97 With C, knit.
ROW 98 With C, k2, p to last 2 sts, k2.
ROW 99 With A, knit.
ROW 100 With A, k2, p to last 2 sts, k2.
ROWS 101 AND 102 Rep rows 99 and 100.
ROWS 103 AND 104 With C, knit.
ROW 105 With B, k1, *sl 1 wyib, k1; rep from * to end.
ROW 106 With B, k1, *sl 1 wyif, k1; rep from * to end.
ROWS 107 AND 108 With C, knit.
ROW 109 With A, k2, *sl 1 wyib, k1;
rep from * to last st, k1.
ROW 110 With A, k2, *sl 1 wyif, p1;
rep from * to last 3 sts, sl 1 wyif, k2.
ROWS 111–114 Rep rows 99 and 100 twice.
ROWS 115 AND 116 Rep rows 97 and 98.
Rep rows 1–116 four times more. Bind off.
Block lightly to measurements.

EMBROIDERY (OPTIONAL)

With tapestry needle and 2 strands of C held tog, work
a French knot above alternate slipped sts in each Row 52.
With 2 strands of B held tog, work a French knot above
alternate slipped sts in each Row 106.
With A, sew cast-on and bound-off edges tog. ◆

Briarclift

TEXTURED PULLOVER

Designed by Jo Allport

INTERMEDIATE

SIZES
Sized for Small (Medium, Large, X-Large).
Shown in size Small.

YARN
Mechita by Malabrigo 3½oz/100g hanks,
each approx 420yd/384m (superwash merino wool)
5 (5, 6, 6) hanks in #682 Poipu

NEEDLES
One pair each sizes 2, 3 and 5 (2.75, 3.25 and 3.75mm)
needles OR SIZES TO OBTAIN GAUGES.

NOTIONS
• Cable needle (cn)
• Stitch holders
• Clip-on st markers
• Tapestry needle

MEASUREMENTS
Bust 37 (40, 43½, 45)"/94 (101.5, 110.5, 117)cm
Length 24¼ (24¾, 25¼, 25¾)"/61.5 (63, 64, 65.5)cm
Upper arm 13¼ (14½, 15, 16)"/33.5 (37, 38, 40.5)cm

GAUGE
29 sts and 38 rows = 4"/10cm over St st
using size 3 (3.25mm) needles; over garter st using
size 2 (2.75 mm) needles.
TAKE TIME TO CHECK YOUR GAUGE.

STITCH GLOSSARY
3-ST RC Sl 2 sts to cn and hold to *back*, k1, k2 from cn.
3-ST LC Sl 1 st to cn and hold to *front*, k2, k1 from cn.

NOTES
To dec on RS rows, ssk at beg of rows and k2tog at end;
on WS rows, p2tog at beg of row and p2tog tbl at end.
Follow the chart for the appropriate needle size to be used
for each of the pattern sts. If it is necessary to change
needles in order to get your gauge, begin with the St st
gauge and then adjust the other needle sizes accordingly,
that is, go up 2 sizes for the cable rows 5–18 and go down
one size for the garter st.

BACK

With size 2 (2.75mm) needles,
cast on 134 (146, 158, 164) sts.
ROW 1 (RS) *K1, p1; rep from * to end.
Rep row 1 for k1, p1 rib for 2½"/6.5cm.
Change to size 3 (3.25mm) needles.

BEGIN CHART PATTERN

ROW 1 (RS) K1 (selvage st), work the 6-st rep to last st,
end k1 (selvage st).
ROWS 2–4 Cont to foll chart in this way with size 3
(3.25mm) needles.
ROWS 5–18 With size 5 (3.75mm) needles, k1,
work the 6-st rep to last st, end k1 (selvage st).
ROWS 19–22 With size 3 (3.25mm) needles, k1,
work the 6-st rep to last st, end k1.
ROWS 23–30 With size 2 (2.75mm) needles, knit.
Rep these 30 rows of chart pat for 3 more reps
or for a total of 120 rows.
Then, cont with size 3 (3.25mm) needles and working
in St st *only*, work even until piece measures 16¼"/41cm
from beg.

ARMHOLE SHAPING

Bind off 4 (5, 6, 6) sts at beg of next 2 rows.
Dec 1 st each side *every* row 3 times. Then, dec 1 st each
side of next row then every other row 5 (8, 10, 10) times
more—108 (112, 118, 124) sts. Work even until armhole
measures 5½ (6, 6½, 7)"/14 (15, 16.5, 18)cm.

NECK SHAPING

NEXT ROW (RS) K23 (25, 28, 31), sl center 62 sts to a st
holder, join a 2nd ball of yarn and k rem 23 (25, 28, 31)
sts. Working both sides at once, dec 1 st at each neck edge
on next WS row, by p2tog tbl on first side and p2tog on
2nd side, then every other row 4 times more—18 (20, 23,
26) sts rem each side. Work even, until armhole measures
7½ (8, 8½, 9)"/19 (20.5, 21.5, 23)cm.

SHOULDER SHAPING

Bind off 6 (6, 7, 8) sts from each shoulder edge once,
then 6 (7, 8, 9) sts twice.

FRONT

Work same as back until armhole measures
3¾ (4¼, 4¾, 5¼)"/9.5 (10.5, 12, 13.5)cm.

NECK SHAPING

NEXT ROW (RS) K28 (30, 33, 36), sl center 52 sts
to a st holder, join a 2nd ball of yarn and k rem
28 (30, 33, 36) sts. Working both sides at once, dec 1 st
at each neck edge on next WS row, by p2tog tbl on first
side and p2tog on 2nd side, then every other row 9 times
more—18 (20, 23, 26) sts rem each side. Work even until
armhole measures same as back.

SHOULDER SHAPING

Work same as for back shoulder shaping.

SLEEVES

With size 2 (2.75 mm) needles, cast on 68 (74, 80, 86) sts.
Work in k1, p1 rib as for back for 2"/5cm. Change to size
3 (3.25mm) needles.

BEG CHART PATTERN

ROW 1 (RS) K1 (selvage st), work the 6-st rep to last st,
end k1 (selvage st).
ROWS 2–120 Work foll chart as on back, changing needle
sizes as indicated, AT SAME TIME, inc 1 st each side of row
7 (by M1 inside of selvage sts) then every 8th row
14 (15, 15, 15) times more—98 (106, 112, 118) sts.
When all 120 rows (or 4 reps of the chart pat) have been
completed, work in St st with size 3 (3.25mm) needle until
piece measures 18"/45.5cm from beg.

CAP SHAPING

Bind off 4 (5, 6, 6) sts at beg of next 2 rows. Dec 1 st each
side *every* row 8 times. Dec 1 st each side of next (RS) row,
then every other row 6 (9, 11, 14) times more—60 sts.
Dec 1 st each side *every* row 8 times—44 sts.
Bind off 14 sts at beg of next 2 rows. Bind off rem 16 sts.

FINISHING

Block pieces to measurements. Sew left shoulder seam.

TURTLENECK

With RS facing and size 5 (3.75mm) needles, pick up
and k15 sts from shaped back neck edge, k62 sts from
back neck holder, pick up and k15 sts from shaped back
neck edge, 25 sts from shaped front neck edge, k52 sts
from front neck holder, pick up and k25 sts from shaped
front neck edge—194 sts. Work in k1, p1 rib for 2"/5cm.
Change to size 3 (3.25mm) needles and work in rib for
4"/10cm more. Change to size 2 (2.75mm) needles and
work in rib until turtleneck measures 8"/20.5cm.
Bind off in rib. Sew right shoulder and turtleneck seam.
Set in sleeves. Sew side and sleeve seams.
Using tapestry needle, weave in ends on the WS. ◆

CHART PATTERN

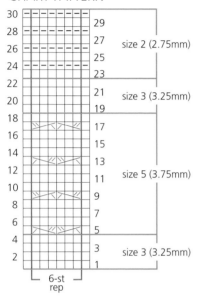

Chart rows (bottom to top), with needle sizes noted:

- size 3 (3.25mm): rows 1–3
- size 5 (3.75mm): rows 5–17
- size 3 (3.25mm): rows 19–21
- size 2 (2.75mm): rows 23–29

6-st rep

STITCH KEY

- ☐ k on RS, p on WS
- ⊟ p on RS, k on WS
- 3-st RC
- 3-st LC

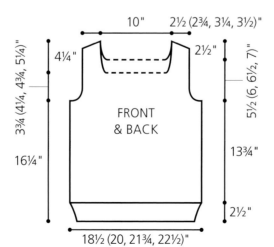

FRONT & BACK

- 10"
- 2½ (2¾, 3¼, 3½)"
- 4¼ "
- 2½ "
- 3¾ (4¼, 4¾, 5¼)"
- 5½ (6, 6½, 7)"
- 13¾ "
- 16¼ "
- 2½ "
- 18½ (20, 21¾, 22½)"

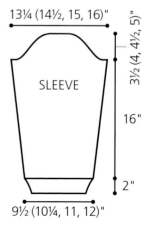

SLEEVE

- 13¼ (14½, 15, 16)"
- 3½ (4, 4½, 5)"
- 16 "
- 2"
- 9½ (10¼, 11, 12)"

Kenilworth

THRUMMED MITTENS

Designed by Hannah Wallace

INTERMEDIATE

YARN

Mechita by Malabrigo, 3½oz/100g hank,
each approx 420yd/384m (superwash merino wool)
• 1 hank in #666 Paprika (A)
Rasta by Malabrigo, 5.3oz/150g hanks,
each approx 90yd/82m (merino wool) {6}
• 1 hank in #023 Pagoda (B)

NEEDLES

• One set (4) each size 2 (2.75mm) and size 3 (3.25mm)
double-pointed needles (dpn), OR SIZE TO OBTAIN GAUGE

NOTIONS

• Stitch marker
• Stitch holder

MEASUREMENTS

Wrist circumference (unstretched) 5"/13cm
Length 9¼"/23.5cm

GAUGE

26 sts and 34 rows = 4"/10cm over St st
using size 3 (3.25mm) needles and A.
TAKE TIME TO CHECK YOUR GAUGE.

MAKE THRUMS

NOTE It is helpful to prepare several thrums ahead of time.
With B, cut several 5"/12.5cm pieces.
Separate each piece lengthwise into 2 or 3 smaller strands.
Turn ends to center and twist to secure.

STITCH GLOSSARY

THRUM STITCH Insert RH needle under bar between
sts from front to back. Fold thrum in half and loop over
right hand needle. Holding ends of thrum to keep
them even, pull loop forward under bar. Knit foll stitch
on LH needle with A, and pass thrum loop over.
Give thrum ends a tug to tighten.

THRUM PATTERN

(multiple of 4 sts)
RND 1 *K3, thrum st; rep from * around.
RNDS 2–5 Knit.
RND 6 *K1, thrum st, k2; rep from * around.
RNDS 7–10 Knit.
Rep rnds 1-10 for thrum pat.

MITTEN

With smaller needles and A, cast on 56 sts.
Divide evenly on 3 dpn (19, 19, 18) and join,
place marker for beg of rnd.
RND 1 *K2, p2; rep from * around.
Rep rnd 1 until cuff measures 2"/5cm.

BEG THRUM PAT
Change to larger dpn. Work thrum pat rnds 1-10 twice.

GUSSET

NOTE Cont thrum pat throughout mitten. Keep as close
to thrum pat as possible while working gusset.
RNDS 1–4 P1, k7, p1, k to end of rnd.
RND 5 P1, k3, M1, k1, M1, k3, p1,
k to end of rnd—58 sts.
RNDS 6–9 P1, k9, p1, k to end of rnd.
RND 10 P1, k4, M1, k1, M1, k4, p1,
k to end of rnd—60 sts.
RNDS 11–14 P1, k11, p1, k to end of rnd.
RND 15 P1, k5, M1, k1, M1, k5, p1,
k to end of rnd—62 sts.
RNDS 16–19 P1, k13, p1, k to end of rnd.
RND 20 P1, k6, M1, k1, M1, k6, p1,
k to end of rnd—64 sts.
RND 21 P1, k15, p1, k to end of rnd.
RND 22 P1, sl 15 sts to holder, cast on 15 sts using
backwards loop method, k to end of rnd—64 sts.
Cont thrum pat until mitten measures 9"/22.5cm from
beg, end with a rnd 4 or 9 of thrum pat.

TOP SHAPING

RND 1 [K1, k2tog] 20 times, k4—44 sts.
RND 2 Work rnd 1 or 6 of thrum pat as established.
RND 3 Knit.
RND 4 [K1, k2tog] 14 times, k2tog—29 sts.

RND 5 [K2tog] 14 times, k1—15 sts.
RND 6 [K2tog] 7 times, k1—8 sts.
Cut yarn, leaving a tail. Thread tail through rem sts,
draw tog and secure end.

THUMB
SET-UP RND Slip 15 sts from holder to larger dpn.
Pick up and k 15 sts from cast on edge around thumb
opening—30 sts.
NEXT RND [K13, k2tog] twice—28 sts.
Work in thrum pat until thumb measures 2½"/6cm.

TOP SHAPING
DECREASE RND *K2tog; rep from * around—14 sts.
Rep decrease rnd every rnd until 4 sts rem.
Cut yarn, leaving a tail. Thread tail through rem sts,
draw tog and secure end.
Work second mitten in same way. ◆

Dorilton

LACE HAT

Designed by Alexandra Davidoff Studio

INTERMEDIATE

YARN

Sock by Malabrigo, 3½oz/100g hanks,
each approx 440yd/402m (superwash merino wool)
• 1 hank in #855 Aguas

NEEDLES

• One each sizes 1 and 3 (2.25 and 3.25mm)
circular needles each 16"/40cm long,
OR SIZE TO OBTAIN GAUGE
• One set (5) each size 3 (3.25mm)
double-pointed needles (dpn)

NOTIONS

• Stitch markers
• Cable needle (cn)

MEASUREMENTS

• Circumference 18"/45.5cm
• Length 9½"/24cm

GAUGE

26 sts and 38 rounds = 4"/10cm over St st
using size 3 (3.25mm) needles.
TAKE TIME TO CHECK YOUR GAUGE.

STITCH GLOSSARY

2-ST RPC Sl 1 to cn, hold to *back*, k1, p1 from cn.
2-ST LPC Sl 1 to cn, hold to *front*, p1, k1 from cn.

LACE PATTERN

NOTE Lace pattern may be worked from text or
chart. Repeat begins with 10 sts and st count varies
as pattern is worked.
(multiple of 10 sts, inc'd to 14, dec'd to 10)
RND 1 *P4, k1, [yo, k1] twice, p3; rep from * around.
RND 2 *P4, k5, p3; rep from * around.
RND 3 *P3, 2-st RPC, k1, [yo, k1] twice, 2-st LPC, p2;
rep from * around.
RND 4 *P3, k1, p1, k5, p1, k1, p2; rep from * around.
RND 5 *P2, 2-st RPC, p1, k5, p1, 2-st LPC, p1;
rep from * around.
RND 6 *P2, k1, p2, k5, p2, k1, p1; rep from * around.
RND 7 *P1, 2-st RPC, p2, ssk, k1, k2tog, p2, 2-st LPC;
rep from * around.

RND 8 *P1, k1, p3, k3, p3, k1; rep from * around.
RND 9 *K2, p3, S2KP, p3, k1; rep from * around.
RND 10 *K2, p7, k1; rep from * around.
RND 11 *[Yo, k1] twice, p7, k1; rep from * around.
RND 12 *K4, p7, k1; rep from * around.
RND 13 *K1, [yo, k1] twice, 2-st LPC, p5, 2-st RPC; rep from * around.
RND 14 *K5, p1, k1, p5, k1, p1; rep from * around.
RND 15 *K5, p1, 2-st LPC, p3, 2-st RPC, p1; rep from * around.
RND 16 *K5, p2, k1, p3, k1, p2; rep from * around.
RND 17 *Ssk, k1, k2tog, p2, 2-st LPC, p1, 2-st RPC, p2; rep from * around.
RND 18 *K3, p3, k1, p1, k1, p3; rep from * around.
RND 19 *S2KP, p3, k3, p3; rep from * around.
RND 20 *P4, k3, p3; rep from * around.
Rep rnds 1–20 for lace pat

HAT

With smaller circular needle, cast on 140 sts. Join, taking care not to twist sts, and place marker for beg of rnd.
RND 1 *K1 tbl, p1; rep from * around.
Rep rnd 1 for k1 tbl, p1 rib for 1½"/4cm.
Change to larger circular needle.

BEG LACE PAT

Work rnds 1–20 of lace pat 3 times,
then rep rnds 1–9 once more—140 sts.

CROWN SHAPING

NOTE Change to dpn when sts no longer fit comfortably on circular needle.
DEC RND 1 [K2tog, p7, k1] 14 times—126 sts.
NEXT RND [K1, p7, k1] 14 times.
DEC RND 2 [Ssk, p5, k2tog] 14 times—98 sts.
NEXT RND [K1, p5, k1] 14 times.
DEC RND 3 [Ssk, p3, k2tog] 14 times—70 sts.
NEXT RND [K1, p3, k1] 14 times.
DEC RND 4 [Ssk, p1, k2tog] 14 times—42 sts.
NEXT RND [K1, p1, k1] 14 times.
DEC RND 5 [Ssk, k1] 14 times—28 sts.
NEXT RND Knit.
Cut yarn and pull through rem sts, draw up and secure.
Do *not* block, as it will flatten the leaf pattern. ◆

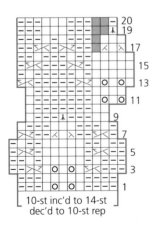

10-st inc'd to 14-st
dec'd to 10-st rep

STITCH KEY

- ☐ k
- ⊟ p
- ⊡ yo
- ⧄ k2tog
- ⧅ ssk
- ⅄ S2KP
- ⧄⧄ 2-st RPC
- ⧅⧅ 2-st LPC
- ▨ no stitch

Abbreviations

KNIT ABBREVIATIONS

approx approximately

beg begin(ning)

CC contrast color

cn cable needle

cm centimeter(s)

cont continue(ing)

dec decrease(ing)

dpn double-pointed needle(s)

foll follow(s)(ing)

g gram(s)

inc increase(ing)

k knit

k2tog knit two stitches together

k3tog knit three stitches together

kfb knit into front and back of stitch

LH left-hand

M1 make one (see Glossary)

MC main color

m meter(s)

mm millimeter(s)

oz ounce(s)

p purl

p2tog purl two stitches together

pat(s) pattern(s)

pm place marker

rem remain(s)(ing)

rep repeat

RH right-hand

rnd(s) round(s)

RS right side

SKP see Glossary

sl slip

sl st slip stich

sm slip marker

ssk slip, slip, knit (see Glossary)

st(s) stitch(es)

St st stockinette stitch (see Glossary)

tbl through back loop

tog together

WS wrong side

wyib with yarn in back

wyif with yarn in front

yd(s) yard(s)

yo yarn over

* repeat directions following * as many times as indicated

[ ] repeat directions inside brackets as many times as indicated

CROCHET ABBREVIATIONS

ch chain

sl st slip stitch

sc single crochet

hdc half-double crochet

dc double crochet

tr treble crochet

Knitting Needles

U.S.	METRIC
0	2mm
1	2.25mm
2	2.75mm
3	3.25mm
4	3.5mm
5	3.75mm
6	4mm
7	4.5mm
8	5mm
9	5.5mm
10	6mm
10½	6.5mm
11	8mm
13	9mm
15	10mm
17	12.75mm
19	15mm
35	19mm

*Note The needle sizes used in this book vary, based on the design and desired drape of the fabric. They may be different than the suggested needle size on the ball band. To achieve the look of the pictured garment, always make a gauge swatch and change the needle size to obtain the gauge given at the beginning of the instructions.

Distributors

USA
Malabrigo
www.malabrigoyarn.com

Europe
Malabrigo
www.malabrigoyarn.com

Canada
Diamond Yarn
www.diamondyarn.com

Finland
Lankatalo Priima
www.lankatalopriima.com

Russia
Praimar Hobby, LLC
www.vk.com/malabrigo

Sweden
Hamilton Designs
www.corneliahamilton.com

BIG SELLERS

Hana Trading Co.
42-472 Ihyeondong
Seogu, Daegu
Korea

Gosyo Co. Ltd.
20 Nishikanemaru, Kita gata-cho
Ichicomiya City, Aichi Pref.
Japan 493-8001

*Note Be sure to get enough yarn to complete your project since each bag is a different dye lot, and skeins may vary from bag to bag. In the tagged (*) colors, the skeins may vary one from the other even within the same bag. To ensure random color distribution, work from two balls of yarn at once, alternating a few rows from each ball.

Glossary

Garter stitch Knit every row. For circular knitting: Alternate knit one round, purl one round.

Make one Insert tip of LH needle from front to back under the strand between the last stitch worked and the next stitch on the needle. Knit into the back loop to increase one stitch.

SKP slip 1, knit 1, pass slip stitch over knit 1—1 st dec'd.

SK2P slip 1, knit 2 stitches together, pass slip stitch over k2tog—2 sts dec'd.

ssk Slip next two sts knitwise, one at a time, to right-hand needle. Insert tip of left-hand needle into fronts of these sts from left to right and knit them together—1 st dec'd.

St st Knit right-side rows and purl wrong-side rows. For circular knitting: Knit all rounds.

CREDITS PHOTOGRAPHER: Rose Callahan HAIR AND MAKEUP: Nickee David CREATIVE DIRECTOR: Diane Lamphron TECHNICAL EDITORS: Carla Scott, Loretta Dachman, Mari Lynn Patrick, Renee Lorion FASHION STYLIST: Josefina Garcia YARN COORDINATOR: Jaclene Sini